HOW TO
TRAUMATIZE YOUR CHILDREN

THE *Self-Hurt* SERIES

KNOCK KNOCK
VENICE, CALIFORNIA

Published by
Knock Knock
1633 Electric Avenue
Venice, CA 90291
www.knockknock.biz

Illustrated by Mark Weber

ISBN: 978-160106038-9
UPC: 8-25703-50100-1

CONTENTS

CHAPTER 1
INTRODUCTION:
TRAUMA WITH A PURPOSE

ALL CHILDREN NEED A STEADY DOSE of trauma in order to conduct therapy-worthy adult lives. While most—if not all—parents traumatize their children accidentally, the fact that you're reading this book shows that you love your kids so much that you'll screw them up deliberately and with skill. Rather than mindlessly repeating the trauma that was visited upon you by your own parents, you know the value of seeking improvement from one generation to the next. You understand that children need psychological peril they can take with them into adulthood and all future relationships, and you care enough to do it yourself. With this book and a bit of focus, you'll be traumatizing your children in no time. You'll learn:

- How the advantages of childhood trauma will benefit your children.

- Dynamics common to most traumatic parenting and how to amplify them in your own parent-child interactions.

- How to play to your own strengths in choosing a particular traumatizing approach, based on your natural inclinations and behavioral style.

- For each traumatizing philosophy, what outcomes to expect in your children, both immediately and when they grow into adulthood.

Trauma Denial:
It's Not Just a River in Egypt

The secret truth of trauma is that *all* children are traumatized, no matter their parents' efforts to the contrary. If a parent tries to avoid the strictness of her own upbringing, she will visit inappropriate lenience upon her offspring. The differences between inadvertently traumatizing your children and doing so purposefully are as follows:

1. You will choose your traumatizing style based on your family's needs rather than defaulting into it by instinct.

2. The trauma will be more skillfully applied, with mid-course corrections possible thanks to self-awareness.

3. Because trauma is inevitable, you won't spin in circles of self-recrimination as you attempt to avoid it.

4. Unhampered by denial, you won't be surprised when your children turn out to be screwed up. Rather than asking "Where did I go wrong?" you'll know exactly what you did right.

"My Parents Were Crazy" The Many Benefits of Trauma

The traumatized child becomes a rich, flavorful adult, equipped with resources that untraumatized or mistraumatized children don't possess. While your child may initially rebel against your traumatizing style, someday he will be not only be grateful, he will possibly choose to replicate it with his own offspring. Merely by reading this book, you most likely already believe in the importance of trauma. In your parenting journey, however, you will no doubt encounter naysayers and know-it-alls, so it's always useful to be equipped with as many counterarguments as possible.

Your Child Will Fit In

Because everybody is traumatized in childhood, your child will experience belonging and acceptance. During adolescence, for example, your child could forge friendships of rebellion, experimenting with sex, drugs, and piercings alongside her peers. In adulthood, your child will be able to discuss with friends his repetitive dysfunctional relationships, wondering aloud why it is that he seeks out the same noncommittal bimbos over and over again.

Your Child Will Have Character

Regular adversity is like a Thigh Master for the inner self, and the strength arising from trauma is a hallmark of the successfully screwed-up adult. The rare child who has not been traumatized has trouble handling the realities of a cruel world, and may crumble at the first sign of trouble. The traumatized child, on the other hand, meets the world with well-developed muscles, prepared with such tools as selfishness, lack of boundaries, or a tough outer-shell. Despite idealized notions to the contrary, a traumatized child is a prepared child.

Your Child Will Have Something to Rebel Against

While not all traumatizing approaches result in rebellion, many do. What object is better to rebel against than a loving parent? In addition to being a virtually universal rite of passage, rebellion allows your child to experiment with alternate world-views, fashion statements, and addictions. As a parent, you get to watch your child spread her wings and crash, and even perhaps come crawling back to you to acknowledge that you were right after all.

Your Child Will Hate You

The psychological life cycle dictates that children should hate their parents. Think back on your childhood—

your parents really did a number on you, right? Of course they did—it's exactly what parents are *supposed* to do. Because you love your kids, you know they deserve torture and torment. Whether you make your child suffer in exactly the same way as you did or choose a new methodology, it's your responsibility to perpetuate this precious gift of intergenerational animosity.

Your Child Will Need Therapy

Those who pooh-pooh therapy tend to be so mired in denial and judgment that they don't possess the courage to explore their innermost selves. Thus it falls to those who have been traumatized to seek out this resource, because if individuals are not in enough pain,

Americans Are Top Traumatizers!

According to UNICEF, the United States is the second best place in the world to traumatize children, topped only by England (those darn Brits). A 2007 study of developed countries revealed that the American youths are global leaders in poor diets, excessive weight, low physical activity levels, and infrequent family dinners. The United States also set the pace for high exposure to violence and bullying, not to mention the high number of 15-year-olds who smoke, drink, and have sex. God bless America!

they will never willingly choose to attend the university of the inner self. Resources for the traumatized abound, from psychoanalysis to self-help groups to psychotropic medications. The successfully traumatized can avail themselves of institutionalization, electroshock therapy, and rebirthing. Those who do not believe themselves to be traumatized will never reach out to this richly arrayed support system, sentencing them to live a life that is both less aware and less colorful.

Your Child Will Be Interesting and Creative

It's well known at this point that most creative individuals were deeply traumatized. Your traumatized child may become a painter, musician, or graffiti artist, or might even write a memoir, the high watermark of trauma. When your child releases a memoir about her childhood, you know you've done your job as a parent.

Your Child Will Traumatize Her Own Children

In being parented, children learn to parent. How can you expect your offspring to properly raise their own children without the benefit of solid role models? Since, as stated above, trauma is inevitable, the deliberately traumatized child will grow up to be the kind of thoughtful parent you yourself want to be. When you reach the grandparenting stage of your life, you will sit on the front porch secure in the knowledge that you did your job, able to watch with pride as your grandchildren misbehave.

Overcoming Obstacles to Traumatizing Your Children

While traumatizing your children is beyond a doubt the best parenting choice, like any worthwhile endeavor, it's not necessarily easy. If you're armed with the knowledge of what to expect, however, you can anticipate

Bumper-Sticker Love

Proclaiming your parental pride on the bumper of your car (preferably a mini-van or SUV) is one of the most meaningful ways to show your children how much you care. Until recently, there was little bumper-sticker choice for trauma-inducing parents; instead, brainwashed parents mindlessly posted the mass-distributed bumper stickers given out by their children's teachers to publicize their schools. Fortunately, there's a new movement afoot in bumper-sticker poetry, one that celebrates the trauma we so skillfully inflict:

- My hockey mom can beat up your soccer mom.
- My honor student fired your stupid kid.
- My kid beat up your honor student.
- My kid had sex with your honor student.
- Proud parent of a stupid kid.
- My kid can let himself in the door, cook dinner, and read himself a bedtime story.
- My kid sells term papers to your honor student.
- My kid was asshole of the month.
- My kid was inmate of the month.
- My president can drink your honor student under the table.

problems before they become crises as well as amass the tools with which to address them.

You Didn't Like the Way You Were Traumatized

Many people look back on their own childhood and critique the way their parents traumatized them. While it's tempting to throw the baby out with the bathwater and resolve not to traumatize at all, a more practical approach is to determine a new and different way to traumatize your own children. Fortunately, there is a whole range of traumatizing techniques from which to choose. While it's perhaps easier to traumatize your children in the exact same way as you yourself were traumatized—indeed, this is the instinctive but ill-considered strategy of most parents—with the help of this book, you can reinvent your own traumatic parenting style out of love for your children. You don't have to be imprisoned by your childhood—you can be empowered by it.

Traumatizing Your Children Is Hard Work

There's no question that parenting is the toughest job you'll ever love. Once you bring a tiny, helpless life into the world, however, you have a responsibility to traumatize that child to the best of your abilities. While some individuals gravitate naturally toward skillful trauma, others must try a little bit harder. As you adopt your chosen traumatizing style, its approach will slowly become second nature. While the beginning may be challenging, one day you'll realize that you're traumatizing your child in exactly the way you wanted to, seemingly without effort, and all your hard work will pay off. Because your child will have seen how much effort you're putting into the process, he'll feel grateful that you cared enough to traumatize him with deliberate intention.

Doubts About Your Chosen Traumatizing Approach

Because parenting is so challenging, there's no avoiding the fact that some days you will question all you've chosen for your child. Especially in adolescence, your child will throw up in your face everything you've done, questioning your values and actions. When these moments occur, your task is to maintain your own self-confidence, because these reactions are natural and mean you're doing everything right. When it comes to trauma, there's no wrong way, there's only poor execution. With the help of this book and your parental love, you'll traumatize effectively and, inevitable missteps aside, the end result will be a truly screwed-up child.

Criticism from Others

Different parenting approaches can drive wedges between the closest of friends. Even lifelong friendships encounter problems once the children arrive when one person turns out to be an overbearing stage parent while

Everybody Needs Therapy

Psychotherapy and its handmaiden, psychotropic medication, are prerequisites for contemporary wellness. When children grow up without reasons to seek mental help, they find themselves to be out of step with their peers. In the last two years, almost 30 percent of American adults have either seen a mental-health professional or been prescribed a drug for a mood disorder. Of those who claim they've suffered an experience warranting mental-health attention, almost 40 percent have not received treatment. But the statistic most supportive of the decision to traumatize one's children is this: almost half of all adults believe their parents would have benefited from therapy.

the other parents with indulgence and neglect. While it's tempting to critique the way others have chosen to parent, it's best to keep your thoughts to yourself and stay true to your own course. Unfortunately, not all parents will be as diplomatic as

you. Some may criticize the traumatizing approach that you've selected.
In these instances, it's important to
remember that you know what's best
for your child.

A few parents actually believe that
it's possible to avoid traumatizing
their children. In a deluded effort to
parent perfectly, they read books that
profess to teach foolproof methods of
behavior, discipline, and compassion.
Unfortunately, these approaches tend
to discourage the time-honored neces-
sity of trauma and set up unrealistic
expectations for a "healthy" outcome.
When you encounter these naysayers,
don't even try to reason with them—
as a parent, your mantra should be
"Never explain, never justify."

Trauma: Beneficial and Inevitable

While perhaps you've long suspected that traumatizing was the right way to parent, now you've got some tangible evidence on your side. Armed with motivation and resolve, you're on the road to being the best traumatizer you can be. In the next chapter, we'll explore some dynamics that are consistent to all traumatizing approaches so that you can mingle the basics into whatever specific style you determine is appropriate for your family.

CHAPTER 2
BUILDING THE FOUNDATION: DYNAMICS OF UNIVERSAL TRAUMA

WHILE PARENTING FOR MAXIMUM trauma can manifest itself in various styles, there are certain fundamentals that will scar children no matter your approach. The twentieth century was the age of psychology. Ushered in by Sigmund Freud in the late nineteenth century, principles of psychoanalysis had us looking inward in a manner no less revolutionary than such outward travel as journeying into space. Because much of this exploration focused on childhood development, we now have a wealth of information on what exactly traumatizes children. All the principles outlined in this book rely on decades of scholarship, drawing on studies performed both in the laboratory and in the field. While it may be difficult to translate some of these recommendations into behavioral change, you can rest assured that when you do parent according to these principles, you will achieve the desired results. We'll introduce you to such concepts as:

- How parental unreliability can unseat even the healthiest child's self-esteem.

- Why it's so important to practice inconsistency in meting out discipline.

- The dangers of actually listening to your child and responding to her needs.

- Why you and your spouse should always adopt different child-rearing approaches and argue over them frequently.

Unreliability: The Enemy of Security and Trust

Parental unreliability is at the root of the majority of childhood trauma. While unreliability comes easily to some parents, for others it goes against their underlying integrity and must be cultivated with hard work. The larger impact of unreliability is that it erodes trust of all kinds—trust that others will care, trust that others will tell the truth, trust that others will be there when the going gets tough. Indeed, most children who grow up with unreliable parents have difficulty trusting as adults, so your unreliability will set your kids up for a lifetime of dysfunctional and failed relationships.

The most basic form of unreliability starts in early childhood—are you there when your child cries? While the indulgent parent will be there too much, not allowing the child to develop his own forms of self-soothing, and the neglectful parent will almost never be there, the most effective form of unreliability is sometimes to be there and sometimes not. As you will see below, inconsistency is an integral part of traumatic parenting, and over the years inconsistent reliability will translate in your child's memory into out-and-out unreliability. Your child should never know when you will respond to his needs, when he will get a kiss on his boo-boo, when he will be told to buck up and get on with it, or, best of all, when he will be completely ignored.

As your child gets older, you can begin lying to her, demonstrating that people are not to be trusted. In accordance with your child's developmental stages, this will

"Your responsibility as a parent is not as great as you might imagine. You need not supply the world with the next conqueror of disease or major motion-picture star. If your child simply grows up to be someone who does not use the word 'collectible' as a noun, you can consider yourself an unqualified success."

—Fran Lebowitz

start with small fibs, such as the existence of Santa, the Tooth Fairy, and the Easter Bunny; escalate into larger misrepresentations, including a sex talk that points to birds, bees, cabbage patches, and storks; mature into temporal prevarication when you say "I'll be back soon" then go on a three-day bender; and peak when you inform your child, say, that the man who raised her is not, in fact, her real father. While you may feel guilty for lying (indeed, emphasis on honesty for its own sake may be one of the numbers your parents pulled on you), remember that you're fibbing for a higher goal—to damage your child's ability to trust.

One form of lying is so important that it merits its own discussion: parental follow-through. To truly set up your children for lifetimes of mistrust and insecurity, you'll want to be sure that you rarely follow through on your promises. Whether you assure your child that he will receive a reward or that you will pick him up after soccer practice, it must be anybody's guess as to whether you will actually make good on your commitment. If you keep your child off-guard in the most primary of relationships, by the time he is an adult, he will have completely lost the ability to trust and will most likely be untrustworthy himself.

Dr. Jekyll or Mr. Hyde? Fostering Unpredictability

The successfully traumatized child should never know what kind of home or situation she is walking into, and she should have no idea what kind of response her behavior will garner. One of the best ways to cultivate this environment is to allow yourself to express wide swings of mood. For those who are naturally even-keeled, this may prove challenging, but it's easily accomplished by working yourself up into a tizzy about something totally irrelevant then taking it out on your children. One afternoon your kids should come home to find a nurturing parent who's curious about what happened at school. The next day, they should encounter a parent who's racing around the house in a manic rage, angry at them through no fault of their own,

Traumatic Intentions

For many of the most prevalent traumatizing approaches, the acceptance trend is on the upswing. According to a recent survey by market research firm Synovate, 43 percent of parents would like to be best friends with their offspring (see chapter 7, "We Share Everything: Parent as Best Friend"), and 40 percent would buy their children everything they wanted if it was within their means (see chapter 6, "Whatever They Want: Indulgence Begets Entitlement").

This parallels an evolution in the way we view children's roles in our lives (similar to our contemporaneous shift toward parenting and spoiling our housepets). According to sociology professor Sampson Lee Blair, families used to view children as "financial assets" necessary to help out on the farm. Now, however, parents interact with their children as "emotional assets, the objects of their love and affection."

As outlined in chapter 10, "Enjoying Your Legacy of Trauma," however, the next generation will choose different ways to traumatize their offspring. Of the teens and young adults polled by Synovate, only 28 percent plan to be best friends with their children and only 10 percent would buy their kids everything they desired.

evincing no concern whatsoever for what transpired at school. Each parent's version of these scenarios will differ; the important thing to remember is that your children should never be able to guess what awaits them behind the house or car door.

Beyond your larger moods, you should never respond to your child in a predictable way. If your child gets a C+, for example, try to pitch a fit one semester, grounding him for two weeks, and the next semester let him know that you understand that he tried his best. This will nurture your child's fear of the unknown, and gradually he will start hiding things from you and declining to seek your counsel, both of which will point him in ever more problematic life directions.

Consistent Inconsistency

Nothing keeps a child on her toes like inconsistency. In a child's earliest years, this should manifest itself in a lack of routine. Regular mealtimes and bedtimes are anathema to the traumatized child—avoid them strenuously, frequently changing the protocol. Some days you'll want to bathe your child in the morning, while other times she'll get a bath right before bed. Routine is one of the surest ways to stunt your child's traumatization, so it is to be avoided at all costs.

When it comes to discipline and expectations for your child's behavior, you'll want to practice setting rules only to break them. The old saying "Do as I say, not as I do" will be your guiding principle. For example, during the teen years, you will want to forbid your child from drinking to excess while flaunting your drinking at every turn. If you hold your child to certain standards that you cannot live up to yourself, your child will become sneaky and hypocritical, knowing there is wiggle room in every standard.

Like unreliability and unpredictability, inconsistency has the added virtue of undermining any child's faith in the constancy of the world. Because no stimulus will ever garner the same response, your child will learn that nothing is to be trusted.

There is one exception to the rule of inconsistency, however: overly rigid parenting that fails to take into account anything about the child herself will also provide trauma and torment, generally resulting in a child who cannot think for herself.

Branding Them for Life

One of the very first acts of parenthood is choosing a name that will accompany a child throughout his life. Why pass up this opportunity to scar your child deeply and repeatedly?

If you prefer the traditional route, select a name that many of your child's peers will also have. Whether you're inspired by a book such as *Beyond Jennifer & Jason, Madison & Montana* or you surf the Internet for top rankings, an overly common name will help your child feel that he doesn't have his own identity and will assure that he must use his last initial in school.

In another direction, you can follow in the footsteps of trend-setting celebrities by inventing something unique or just plain weird, such as star-offspring monikers Pilot Inspektor, Heavenly Hiraani Tiger Lily, Kal-el, or Moon Unit. If you're drawn to the narcissist parenting type (see chapter 5), name your child after yourself—multiple times, as with boxer George Foreman's five sons.

If you're uncertain how best to traumatize your child on his birth certificate, however, you can hire a child-naming consultant, newly anointed professionals who understand that *everything* today is a brand—including your child's name.

Your Child's Cues and Needs: Ignore Them

Your parenting approach should have nothing whatsoever to do with what your child actually wants or needs. You are the parent, you know best, and your needs come first. You want to determine your traumatic parenting style and stick with it, even if your individual children are very different from one another.

Throughout their lives, children will give you cues, some of them subtle and others quite overt. Your job is to second-guess those messages or, best of all, not hear them. If you do accidentally happen to receive a signal, you can either ignore it or, in an alternatively effective approach, ridicule it. For example, if your child is behaving in a needy way, the last thing you should do is reassure her. Instead, go about your own business, and if she persists in communicating her needs, make fun of her by calling attention to her immaturity.

By not listening to your children, they will develop insecurities about their worthiness and whether or not they know their own minds. They will second-guess their instincts and behave as doormats in relationships. Sooner or later, they will stop expressing themselves entirely. Or, they could become bombastic know-it-alls out of fear that no one will listen to them as adults.

As with the rule of inconsistency, there is one exception to the principle of discounting your child's needs, and like inconsistency, that exception falls into the category of an extreme. Parents who indulge a child's every utterance, as you will see in chapter 6, will traumatize that child just as surely as if they had ignored her.

Warring Parenting Styles: 'Til Death Do You Part

For children who are lucky enough to have both parents involved in their upbringing, whether those parents are married or divorced, the most effective path to trauma lies in each parent having a different approach to child rearing. If both of you are working with this book, you'll want to choose different approaches. This duality not only exposes the child to a broader range of parenting styles, it increases inconsistency, one of the most important trauma principles. Finally, when two parents are not "on the same page," the resulting fighting and hostility ratchets the trauma quotient a few notches higher.

As parents, you never want to present a united front to your children. The most common and intuitive form of this

Cinematic Traumatic Parenting

When getting into the traumatizing mindset, it can be helpful to experience depictions of others who have successfully embodied the role you seek to emulate:

Controller

- *The Great Santini*
- *Mommie Dearest*

Pusher

- *Dead Poets Society*
- *The Turning Point*

Narcissist

- *Mermaids*
- *The Squid and the Whale*

Indulger

- *Clueless*
- *Willy Wonka and the Chocolate Factory*

Best Friend

- *The Professional*
- *Thirteen*

Self-Esteem Killer

- *Cinderella*
- *Now, Voyager*

Neglector

- *American Beauty*
- *Home Alone*

parenting technique manifests as "good cop, bad cop." When one parent is punishing a child, the other eases the pain of discipline with a treat. If one parent enforces a homework regimen, the other parent will propose a last-minute weeknight game of miniature golf. While "good cop, bad cop" is well known, it's not the only such combination. For example, one of you could be controlling while the other systematically crushes self-esteem, or one of you could be indulgent while the other pushes for a national title in figure skating. The options are endless as long as the parents make sure their efforts never duplicate or reflect one another.

The Seven Parenting Styles: Which One Suits You?

While it's critical to understand the foundational principles of traumatic child-rearing, the meat of this book lies in the seven distinct parenting styles. Any parent will do best with an approach that suits his or her personality. By going against your grain, you will sentence yourself to an uphill battle. Children have excellent intuition, and they will suspect that your parenting is not authentic. That's not to say, however, that the seven styles are mutually exclusive. On the contrary, each has much to learn from the others, and would not be without precedent to combine all of them into one supernova approach to traumatic parenting. Therefore you should not jump ahead to the style you think may be yours; instead, take the time to read through and consider them all. Perhaps you'll surprise yourself by choosing another style, or at the very least, you'll have more tools in your kit for the complex, lifelong challenge that is parenting.

CHAPTER 3
EXERTING CONTROL: YOUR CHILD, YOUR PROPERTY

AS A CONTROLLING PARENT, YOU know what's right. You know what your child should fear and what she should believe. You have the final say in what your child should wear every day, what friends she should have, and how much food she should put in her mouth. Because there is no room in your universe for your child's ideas or opinions, you save money on art supplies. There are so many advantages to taking complete control over your child's life. Really, what does she know? She's just a kid! While it takes a bit of work to become a controlling parent, the results for your child are so impressive—obedience, rigidity, psychosomatic stomachaches, lack of resourcefulness, a lifetime of discontent—that many parents consider these techniques to be worth the effort. In this chapter, we'll show you:

- What kinds of people are best suited to exercising dissent-free control.

- Why kids don't need to play, anyway.

- How cell phones and leashes can extend your reach.

- Why to crack down hard on eventual rebellion.

Should You Be a Controller?

The controller is a special type of parent, best suited to individuals with leadership skills and a strong perfectionist drive, generally undergirded by a stimulating combination of failed dreams and entrenched self-loathing. An estimated 50 percent of controlling parents were themselves controlled by their own parents, giving a leg up to those who enjoyed this type of upbringing but far from ruling out those who did not.

The advantages to controlling your child are plentiful. When children are young, they tend not to talk back, and you can quickly squash any backtalk with punishment, criticism, and threatened withholding of love and affection. You'll save yourself the inconvenience of having to deal with gray areas and your child's indecision—for example, an hour-long morning debate about the comparative merit of the pink versus the purple tights could be resolved in mere seconds with white tights, which happen to be the only ones currently available.

While it requires diligence to control to this degree, it also makes your job easier because it results in early-stage obedience. In his teen years, your child may rebel, but at that point you can send him away to "wilderness camp" or a "working ranch." Some of these "educational" opportunities even take place in other countries, allowing your child to see the world as well as permitting you to skirt pesky American laws against corporal punishment.

Controlling cross-pollinates well with a few other traumatic parenting types—the pusher, the narcissist, and the self-esteem killer—though its tools of manipulation and domination can inform all parenting approaches. The basic rule of thumb is, if it irritates you or you have an opinion on it, take control.

You will naturally gravitate toward control if you exhibit any of the following characteristics, behaviors, or beliefs, whether in parenting or in other aspects of your life, such as work or marriage:

- Everything must be done exactly how you want it or you will do it yourself.

- No one appreciates you or understands that everything you do is for their own good. Above all, they fail to realize that the world would fall apart if you weren't holding it all together.

- You believe the world is a dangerous place and you can't do too much to protect your child from harm, even if that means sacrificing freedom.

• Everybody else is stupid.

You Are the Boss

From the moment your child is born, she is a generation younger than you. What does this obvious observation mean? You know better! You have spent a lifetime developing dogma and wisdom, most likely from the school of hard knocks, and by golly, your children will benefit from it. As a parent, your role is to micromanage their every move, and their goal in life is to please you and follow your orders. You did not have children in order to submit to their feeble whims. Instead, your offspring are lumps of clay to be molded in your image. They are lucky to have you as a parent because you know everything.

Your children do not need to waste time—theirs and yours—learning to make decisions on their own or exploring their internal thought processes. Ultimately they will have friends, teachers, professors, bosses, and spouses to make decisions for them, so it doesn't serve their best interests for you to teach them anything other than blind obedience.

Your Children Are Your Property

Not only did you give your children life, you put a roof over their heads and food in their mouths. You pay for toys, orthodontia, and the clothing you pick out for them. All of this adds up to the fact that your children belong to you, body and soul. Until they are 18 or no longer accepting money and housing from you, they must accede to your rules. Remind them frequently of this fact with such statements as, "When *you* pay the bills, *you* make the rules."

When they accept your charity, starting with that baby formula they couldn't get enough of and those pacifiers they carelessly and repeatedly lost, your children relinquish all rights to self-governance, privacy, and choice. You wiped their butts—why wouldn't you read their diaries?

Dissent Is Verboten

Why? Because you said so. What more explanation is required? You are an adult, you know best and are never wrong, and children should respect their parents and accept their leadership blindly. Your children are lucky that they have you to think for them. If your child voices disagreement, it means she is bad and doesn't love

Big Mother

Who needs the stress of keeping a watchful eye on your children? From high- to low-tech, it's never been easier with these devices:

Child safety harness: Like a leash for toddlers, this is the tried-and-true. Now these harnesses come in the form of cuddly stuffed-animal backpacks so you can strap your child in and lead her by the tail!

RFID tag: Children's clothes are now available with radio-frequency identification (RFID) tags, small chip-and-antenna combos. The tags can be encoded with contact and medical information and are traceable within a certain radius. An alarm can be triggered if determined boundaries are breached.

Mobile location service: With GPS technology, parents can pinpoint the location of their child's phone. By programming key areas, such as school or home, parents can be notified when a child arrives at or leaves a location.

Car trackers: Numerous gadgets will now monitor a teen's driving behaviors, including excessive speed, hard braking, and broken curfews or geographical parameters. As an added bonus, parents can retaliate in real time: remotely flashing the car's lights or honking the horn until the teen behaves.

or respect you, in which case you should crack down hard then withhold your love. Whether you call it lip, sass, backtalk, or disrespect, it ranks as one of the most punishable offenses.

When your children disagree with you, tell them they are stupid and ungrateful. Frequently call attention to their status as ignorant youths. Make it clear that you love them when they agree with you. Reversely, if they break the disciple contract, throw a tantrum or give them the silent treatment. Limits and boundaries are clear-cut and nonnegotiable—there are none for you, and many for them. Implement whatever it takes to exercise control, because once your children get the notion that dissent will be tolerated, it's game over for you.

The Motivation of Criticism

Criticism is one of the most useful tools for the controlling parent. Not only does it serve to punish poor behavior as well as reinforce your position as property-owning boss, it undermines their self-confidence so that they believe (correctly) that they couldn't survive without you. A child with poor self-esteem is more easily controlled than one who has developed confidence through praise and independent exploration of the world.

For the controlling parent, praise only comes when a child does exactly what he is told and internalizes your guidance. In order to motivate him to act accordingly, however, you will need criticism to push him on the right track just as gutters serve to punish a poorly thrown bowling ball. Primarily your criticism will center around his intelligence, judgment, and attempts at independent thought, all of which, clearly, are stupid.

Everything Is Dangerous

Your job as a parent is to protect your child from the infinite array of perils while instilling in her the accurate beliefs that people (including friends) are not to be trusted, dogs foam at the mouth, germs lurk on every binky, and life is fatal. These are just a few of the many reasons why your child must not think for herself. There will be no play, because play is how children get hurt. Thanks to modern technology, GPS will accompany your offspring through childhood. Curiosity is bad, all but parent-approved friendships are to be avoided, and antibacterials will be used in all household products, not to mention travel wipes.

By teaching your child about the world's dangers, you will be inspiring the life skill of fear. What should be feared? Everything! Until your child is appropriately apprehensive, you are there to protect her.

Stages of Control

1. **In utero:** Don't submit yourself to the pain and gore of actual labor—plan a

scheduled Cesarean section, whether
or not it's medically recommended,
and deliver your child on the date
you choose.

2. **Infant:** Immediately put your baby on a
schedule that you prefer and let him cry
it out if he doesn't like it.

3. **Baby:** Eating when hungry? That's for
sissies. Instead, enforce a feeding plan
that works for you.

4. **Toddler:** Dictate what your child will
wear, and severely punish tantrums and
expressions of will.

5. **Child:** Don't allow your child to play
outside or choose her own activities and
friends. Plan everything, and enforce the
execution of chores when your child has
an invitation to do something else.

6. **Adolescent:** Your child will start asking to attend boy-girl parties and stay out late, affording you the chance to say no over and over again.

7. **Teen:** The mother lode of control, the teen years offer the opportunity to invade privacy, mock emerging personal taste, and put your child on a diet.

8. **Young adult:** If your child wants your financial support during her college years, she'd darn well better do exactly as you say, including attending the university of your choice.

9. **Adult:** How can you keep control over an adult? Attach strings to everything— gifts, money, and your love. Make your adult children choose between you and their significant others.

Homeschooling: Total Control

The educational gold standard in all-encompass-ing parental control is without a question home-schooling, a movement that's been around as long as there was the option of attending school outside the home. According to the United States Department of Education, the prevalence of homeschooling rose by 29 percent between 1999 and 2006, from 850,000 students to 1.1 million. Parents cited the following top three rea-sons for removing their children from school:

1. Concern about school environment (safety, drugs, and peer pressure): 31 percent.

2. To provide religious or moral instruction: 30 percent.

3. Unsatisfied with the quality of academic instruction available in schools: 16 percent.

With homeschooling, your child will learn only what you want her to know. She won't need to experience the havoc of socialization—the only potential bully at home is you! Because the values you instill will be 100 percent yours, sexuality, drinking, and spiritual questioning will unfold according to your time table. Finally, as a homeschooling parent, you will never have to worry about bomb scares or mass shootings.

Results for the Controlled Child

If you work hard to maintain absolute control over your children, there's so much to look forward to in their adulthood. Your precious offspring will be characterized by the following blessed traits:

- Rigid and uncreative.

- Self-doubting and afraid to take risks.

- Driven to perfection but never satisfied.

- Believe everybody is criticizing or finding fault in them.

- Have difficulty knowing their own emotions.

- Expect others to take advantage of them, because no one is to be trusted.

- Plagued by psychosomatic ailments such as stomachaches and headaches.

- Passive-aggressive, subject to procrastination and resistance.

- Unable to attend to their own needs, instead focusing on others to their own detriment.

- Seek relationships with controlling significant others.

- Prone to eating disorders and addictions.

- Deep down, hate and resent their parents but cannot individuate and separate from them in adulthood.

From Your Loins, Under Your Control

If you find a kindred description in the controlling dynamic, pat yourself on the back and consider yourself fortunate—it's such a rich, diverse approach to parenting! Not only will your child have plenty of damage to repair in adulthood, you'll have the opportunity to reflect on the results of your "I said so" experiment. No one will be able to say that you didn't do it your way, and all results will be attributable to you.

While some parents will adhere to the controlling approach in its entirety, others will take bits and pieces of control while identifying more completely with the other parenting styles. Indeed, that's one of the beauties of the controlling type—it's so universally applicable! Control is most complementary with our next parenting style, the pusher, a brilliant spotlight of enforced success. Read on, and see if this may be the right blend for you!

CHAPTER 4

YOUR CHILD IS AN HONOR STUDENT: PUSHING FOR PERFECTION

WHEN YOU LOOK BACK ON YOUR OWN childhood, just think of how many opportunities were wasted to mold you into a superstar! Most likely your parents didn't realize that they needed to start much earlier to shape you into a world-class ice skater, gymnast, golfer, beauty contestant, pianist, or Harvard student. If they had, who knows what your life would be like now? Fortunately, as a parent yourself, you can live those experiences vicariously as well as give your children the opportunities you never had, all the while basking in the reflected glow of your trophy children's successes.

If you're drawn to pusher parenting, you've got so much to look forward to. From as early as three years old, your child will function as a little professional with you as his manager. Your child will be the blank slate for everything you've ever dreamed about and failed to attain. By pushing your child in everything from sports to music to grades, you are doing him a huge favor, preparing him for a life of success. Pay no attention to whether your child wants these things for himself—what does he know? He's a child!

By the time your child rebels against you and descends into drug addiction and stalled motivation, you will already have several gold medals and trophies in hand to prove that it's not your fault. While it's certainly no walk in the park to carpool, fund, and push your child's way to excellence, the results are well worth it. In this chapter, we'll show you:

- Why your own background and insecurities could provide you with pusher fuel you didn't even know you have.

- Why childhood is for sissies.

- Why you should ask your child to target the unachievable.

- Why public acclaim is so much more important than private fulfillment.

Should You Be a Pusher?

Parents who excel at pushing are often aficionados of public perception. If you always buy the best, care deeply what others think, and enjoy keeping up with the Joneses, you just might have what it takes to be a pusher. Children's achievements are increasingly markers of how well mothers and fathers have plied the parenting trade. If your child does not excel, you yourself are a failure, and everybody will know it.

Pushers believe that children are engineering projects to be subjected to the same efforts one might apply in the workplace. Guided by office tools—calendars, clipboards, spreadsheets—pushers' children's lives bear witness to the complexity of the contemporary age. If your child doesn't distinguish herself, what hope does she have of a successful adulthood?

If you are demanding and perfectionistic, you probably have natural pushing inclinations. For example, one current trend in pushing consists of women who choose to stay at home with their children following high-powered careers. These mothers apply to their children the same talents that got them ahead at work, from tracking milestones to networking to climbing the playground ladder. Another group of pushing pros consist of those who never fully lived out their own fantasies and see their children as another opportunity to do so.

Pushing blends nicely with a few other parenting styles, notably the controller, the narcissist, the indulger, and the self-esteem killer, so if you are an aspiring pusher, pay close attention to those types in order to forge your own unique approach.

You will naturally gravitate toward pushing if you exhibit any of the following characteristics, behaviors, or beliefs, whether in parenting or in other aspects of your life, such as work or marriage:

- What others think of you determines what you think of yourself.

- You sacrifice yourself and work hard toward a higher goal, but that higher goal darn well better come through for you or your efforts will have been wasted.

- Everybody else is the competition.

- There are two types of people in this world: winners and losers.

Train Now:
Childhood Is for Sissies

It used to be that childhood unfolded with little structure. Pre-adults made their way home from school with no extracurricular activities; played whatever games they chose, with whomever they chose; and suffered through long, unplanned summers. Children even got themselves from point A to point B on such mortally dangerous transportation devices as bicycles. It's a wonder anybody from those generations achieved anything at all, let alone survived!

Fortunately, today there's a better way. Now you can plan every second of your child's time to prepare him for real life. We don't get to choose our activities at work, so we would be doing our children a disservice if we were to allow them to chase butterflies and ponder their own imaginations. You'll have no shortage of activities to choose from, thanks to the industries that have developed to improve childhood: tutoring services, Little League, youth soccer, ice-skating coaching, and

Dysfunctional Dictionary

hurried-child syndrome: Condition in which parents overschedule their children's lives, push them hard for academic success, and expect them to behave and react as miniature adults.

hyper-parenting: Child-rearing style characterized by intense parental involvement in managing, scheduling, and enriching all aspects of their children's lives.

trophy child: Child used to impress other people and enhance parental status.

instruction in such areas as art, music, ballet, and martial arts.

Not to mention that all worthwhile endeavors must start young if your child is to have any chance of world-class performance. No award-winning pianist ever started lessons as an adult. Gymnastics is over and done with by one's eighteenth birthday. And Tiger Woods achieved his first hole-in-one at the age of six. As you'll see below, academic success starts even before the child is born, with in utero applications to the right preschool, leading to the right elementary school, leading to Harvard.

Some parents worry needlessly over whether their children actually enjoy their many activities. Who cares? You know best for your child, and if she has any free time in her schedule, you're not doing a good enough job.

Perfection Is the Goal: Setting Your Child Up for Failure

For the pusher, there's no such thing as good enough—there is only perfection. If your child believes it's acceptable to shoot for mediocrity, he'll never live up to his own potential. Because there is always room to do better, the unattainability of perfection and the inevitability of failure will continually motivate your child to do more.

There are numerous antiquated adages that promote middle-of-the-road achievement, focusing on teamwork, doing one's personal best, being a good sport, and learning as you go along. These types of values are the devil's work! In order for your child to get ahead in life, it's critical that you let him know that winning and perfection should be pursued at any cost.

My Child Is an Honor Student: Where's the Plus on that A?

We live in a scholar-eat-scholar world. Your precious child is up against junior Einsteins and baby brain surgeons. By the time your child hits kindergarten, if she's not reading at a fifth-grade level, it's all over for her. As you no doubt know, academic success is now the caste system of contemporary America. If you don't get into the right preschool, with its waiting list longer than your matriculating child's life, you can kiss Harvard goodbye, because one institution feeds right into the next.

Your child should be doing at least an hour of homework daily for each successive grade. Yes, that means she'll be doing 12 hours of homework a day by her senior year of high school, but no one ever promised academic achievement would be easy. If your doctor hasn't called attention to the potential skeletal damage of your child's heavy book bag, then she's not working hard enough.

Some parents are tempted to look at their child's roster of A- grades as "good enough." They don't realize that an A- is the gateway to failure. Soon it'll be a B+, and before you know it, your child will be at a community college planning her "career" in data entry. How will that reflect on you? There's no bumper sticker to celebrate mediocrity.

Academic Doping

Why should you settle for your child's 3.8 GPA? Once solely the domain of adult bodylifters and truck drivers, performance-enhancing drugs have finally become available for kids. Parents are now asking doctors to prescribe ADHD medications such as Ritalin and Adderall to help their children focus on their schoolwork.

According to a 2006 study, two-thirds of physicians reported fielding such requests to the tune of approximately 11 parents per year, and almost 10 percent of the doctors complied. When the physicians deny the requests, they estimate that 16 percent of the parents go on to obtain the drugs without medical approval. With such minor side effects as loss of appetite, irritability, blurry vision, stunted growth, hallucinations, psychotic behavior, and tics and tremors, who wouldn't go the extra distance for their child's success?

Love Is for Winners:
Your Child *Is* His Achievements

If your child believes you will love him no matter what, even if he's a failure, you're doing something wrong. To teach your child that he has intrinsic worth whether or not he succeeds is to prepare him for an idealized world that does not exist. We *are* our successes and our failures—after all, what else is there? As a parent, you need to train your child to live on his own, and if you coddle him with love that he didn't earn, he'll be helpless and lazy once he strikes out on his own. Performance equals love— don't let him think anything different.

Public Acclaim Above All

Performance is the public exhibition of skill, talent, and practice. The answer to the old philosophical question "If a tree falls in the forest and nobody is there to hear it, does it make a sound?" is absolutely not. Why would you spend all those hours in training only to hide your achievements away from the public eye? Our culture is full of reasons to perform, from *Dirty Dancing*'s "No one puts Baby in a corner" to the song "This little light of mine / I'm gonna let it shine."

It's critical that you instill in your children the idea that externally validated success means everything. Internal fulfillment is a luxury most of us can't afford. Yes, we'd all run around with unwaxed legs wearing generic-brand clothing if we could, but what would everybody think? When you are your achievements, the world will sit up and take notice. Your child must know that her accomplishments only mean something if they make you look like a better parent.

Stages of Pushing

1. **In utero:** Play classical music for the fetus by putting Bose headphones on the pregnant belly. Read books on child development and map out your child's future. Apply to preschools.

2. **Infant:** Play books on tape in foreign languages while your infant naps.

3. **Baby:** Teach sign language so your baby can communicate before the speech area of her brain develops.

4. **Toddler:** Put golf clubs, violins, or picture-free books in your child's hands. Call your child "little man" or "little lady" and react to childish behavior with ridicule.

5. **Child:** Expose your child to a wide range of activities until no minute is

unscheduled, or focus your child on only one activity so that he might become world-class.

6. **Adolescent:** Argue with teachers and coaches who want to hold your child back. Hire tutors to compensate for shortcomings at your child's school, and begin prepping for the SATs.

7. **Teen:** Consult a college counselor at the beginning of high school and choose your child's target school. Plot out all the extracurriculars, grades, and advanced-placement courses it will take to get there.

8. **Young adult:** Have your child's college grades sent to your home. If your child did not get into a top school, explore transfer possibilities. Make sure your child maintains her weight.

Go Team!

If your child is an athlete, you can avail yourself of many techniques to assure her wins. Between 2000 and 2003, Frenchman Christophe Fauviau, a true pusher dad, drugged the water bottles of 27 opponents of his tennis-playing teenage son and daughter. Unknowingly sedated by the anti-anxiety drug Temesta, the players (one as young as 11 years old) became weak and nauseous, ensuring victory for Fauviau's children. The last incident resulted in the death of a player who, on the way home from a match, fell asleep at the wheel and crashed into a tree.

Other types of athletes also have impassioned parents behind them. A Massachusetts hockey dad fatally punched another father in the head during his son's scrimmage. The state of Texas is quite the hotspot for pusher parents: in 2005, a disgruntled father shot his son's football coach, and in 1991, a cheerleading mom hired a hitman to take out her daughter's rival's mother so the daughter would not be able to compete.

The best aspect of this type athletic parenting is that children don't even have to be very good players. Fauviau's son, for example, was by all accounts mediocre with the racket, playing matches for purses as small as $50.

9. **Adult:** Hold your child to a rite-of-passage schedule that reflects well on you among your friends: marriage, child-birth, and professional advancement.

Results for the Pushed Child

By pushing your children to achieve perfection, you'll mold adults characterized by the following superstar traits:

- Terrified of making mistakes, avoiding failure rather than targeting success.

- Never satisfied with accomplishments, never good enough, never feel like they measure up.

- Inflexible, risk averse, unplayful, uncreative.

- Prone to anxiety, depression, and psychosomatic complaints.

- Unsuccessful at directing and negotiating their own lives after so much structure.

- Frequently bored and unable to find passion in activities.

- Likely to bow out of pursuits they once worked so hard to master.

- Resentful of their parents.

- Struggles with addiction.

- Anger issues.

Push Them Now, Before It's Too Late

Your children are only with you for a short time, so make the most of it. With all that you've sacrificed to give them every advantage, they should reflect well on you and reaffirm the choice you've made to put them first. If they protest, remember that it's just the short-sighted voice of a child speaking. You know that the long-term rewards will be worth so much more than any short-term discomfort.

Next we'll explore a parenting style that shares some characteristics with the pusher: the parental narcissist. What do you want to see when you look in the mirror of your child's face? Yourself!

CHAPTER 5
IT'S ALL ABOUT YOU: NARCISSISTIC PARENTING

NARCISSISM IS VERY HIP, VERY HOT, very now. Once upon a time, people cared about the community and the world they lived in. Now, however, families more frequently put themselves above the good of the group. It doesn't matter if someone else's Johnny fails school—all they care about is their Joey. Some skilled parents, however, take this typology to a new, individualized level of advancement by actually putting *themselves* ahead of their own children.

Narcissism is the one dynamic that runs through all of the parenting types. When you seek nobly to traumatize others, generally narcissism comes into play somehow.

Whenever a relationship does not take into account the other person's feelings but instead is governed by one person's needs and perceptions, narcissism is present. The controlling parent, for example, is most certainly blessed with a strong dose of narcissism, as are the pusher and the best friend.

In its purest form, however, the glory of narcissism manifests itself as relating everything back to oneself, governed by the true inability to put anybody else's interests first. As you can imagine, this lack of reciprocity makes for a truly fascinating childhood. In this chapter, we'll show you:

- Why your child should come to you and relate to *your* world rather than the other way around.

- Why you should expect your child to praise and compliment you.

- How the threat of abandonment can elicit affection.

- How to lie to your children for your own good.

Should You Be a Narcissist?

If no one adequately appreciates how great you are, odds are good that you're a narcissist and will excel in this parenting type. Your inflated sense of self-importance conflicts somewhat with your need for tribute from others, and if they don't respond appropriately to your contributions, it's necessary for you to punish them in some way.

Narcissistic parents enjoy one of the broadest arenas of traumatic impact because they don't put their children's needs first. As an aspiring narcissist, you should be proud to note that such dynamics infuse all of the other parenting types—indeed, narcissistic parenting takes the traumatic-parenting crown, so if you find yourself in this category, congratulate yourself on your choice!

Narcissistic parents refer all outside events to themselves, interpreting a child's behavior as having been intended to reject, insult, or harm them in some way. Prior to having children, narcissists have experienced this phenomena in other areas—being underappreciated, perceiving others' envy, fielding accusations that they are exploitative, and flying into narcissistic rages. It may have been challenging to conduct mature relationships, with existing interactions characterized by excessive dependence and manipulation.

Fortunately, children adore their parents, so your need for acclaim will be endlessly

> ## Tidings of Trauma
>
> "The first half of our life is ruined by our parents and the second half by our children."
> —Clarence Darrow

satisfied once you've reproduced. Parental narcissism is one of the best ways to get the kudos you so deserve!

You will naturally gravitate toward narcissism if you exhibit any of the following characteristics, behaviors, or beliefs, whether in parenting or in other aspects of your life, such as work or marriage:

- You fantasize about omnipotence.

- You love being the center of attention.

- You find it difficult to understand why others struggle with their petty problems.

- Deep down (unacknowledged to others, of course), you feel defective.

Children Were Born to Love Their Parents

Children have no inherent value other than what they can do for you. Think about all you've sacrificed for them—the sex you had in order to conceive them, pregnancy and delivery, financial outlays and the challenges of keeping them clothed and fed, the fact that they interrupt you all the time and seem to prefer that you weren't drunk. You've done your job and met your end of the bargain. Everything else is up to them.

You *deserve* their love. What child doesn't adore and respect his parents? It's the law of the universe, and if you don't see that filial worship in his eyes, then he's darn well going to feel what it's like to live without his parents' affection. Because you're a super-hero to him, your child must express his love for you with praise—for your personality, your perfume, your outfits, your sex appeal. You gave your child life—now he must learn to meet your ever-shifting emotional needs.

Shut Up! Squelch that Voice

Children are meant to be neither seen nor heard—except when it's convenient or when they're caring for you, reflecting well on you, or boosting your ego in some way. Your child has very little to say about the world—after all, she's just a child! How interesting could she be? Instead, she should be basking in the fascination of your stories and experiences. Indeed, it's vital that you turn every conversation back to yourself. If they've had a bad day at school,

The Mesmerizing Mirror

Many narcissists deny themselves of recognizing their noble tradition and its etymology. The term stems from the Greek myth of Narcissus, the son of a god and a nymph who was renowned for his physical beauty. Though there are a few different renditions of the myth, in the generally accepted version, Narcissus angers the gods by rejecting a romantic interest. As punishment, Narcissus is made to fall in love with his own reflection in the waters of a spring, gazing at himself until he dies. Upon his death, the sweet-smelling flower that bears his name grows in his spot by the waters, drooping its head just as he bowed to see his reflection.

While the story has anti-narcissistic roots, serving as a morality tale warning against self-love, this message is now antiquated. Since the original incident in ancient Greece, no one has died from gazing at themselves in the mirror, except perhaps while driving. Instead, it's useful to understand the story for its psychoanalytic meaning—an ample degree of self-involvement and self-reference. From this perspective, child-rearing can only enhance a parent's life, because children are the ultimate self-reference and function beautifully to reflect the narcissist.

tell them "That's nothing. When I was your age . . ." and make sure they're sympathizing with you by the end of your story.

If your child has an interest or concern that you don't share, ignore her until she returns to a topic that you enjoy. (Indifference is a powerful tool for guiding your children without them knowing it.) Conceptually, you never want to visit your child's world; instead, make her come to yours. You have nothing to learn from her, but she has everything to learn from you. The general rule of thumb is that her interests and hobbies are silly and stupid, but yours are fascinating and worthwhile. Over time, she'll come to agree.

When it is time for your child to feel emotion, don't leave this up to chance. Tell your child what she should feel and don't accept anything different. Counter any attempts at independent feelings by calling her overly sensitive or touchy, and if she persists, go ballistic (see below).

Your Needs Come First

Children like to be the center of attention, but this draws the spotlight away from you. Your child should never be better looking, smarter, or more successful than you. The moment they begin to shine in a way that threatens your stardom, shoot them down. For example, when you play sports or cards, play to win, even if it involves cheating. Anything they can do, you can do better.

When you are in a bad mood or have a headache, your children must not only keep their needs to themselves, they should take care of you. This is especially important if you make the parenting choice to be an alcoholic or other type of addict, as you will require plenty of care, and who better to give it than your kids?

If your children fail to recognize the value of your needs, you'll want to remind them how important you are by bragging about yourself or by teasing or embarrassing them. Soon enough they'll fall in line!

Maintain a Moving Target

As a narcissist, you have an obligation to be inconsistent. Your children should never know what will make you happy and what will send you into a narcissistic rage. As a result, they will feel fragmented, and what's better than a multifaceted personality?

Because morality is relative and deter-mined by you, remember that you are allowed to do whatever you want, whether or not it is "selfish" or "illegal." As a parent, selfishness is your right. Lies are to be used in order to exploit and manipulate children, which is great practice for the exploitation and manipulation you no doubt practice in the outside world.

Above all, your children should understand that they are to do as you say, not as you do. The rules are special for you, and the sooner they grasp that law of the universe, the more they will enjoy the privilege of your "love."

Counter with Contempt

Your children should never forget that your love is conditional. After all, what value would love have if it were guaranteed? If your child toes the line, you will reward him with seductive, charming behavior.

Grabbing the Medical Spotlight

Because children are attention seekers, they frequently pull focus from their parents. One solution to this problem is Munchausen Syndrome by Proxy (MSbP), whereby a parent induces illness in a child in order to receive sympathy from others. In the Eminem song "Cleanin' Out My Closet," for example, the rapper states, "Goin' through public housing systems, victim of Munchausen Syndrome / My whole life I was made to believe I was sick when I wasn't." While some experts dispute the validity of MSbP, there is plenty of anecdotal evidence to support its utility as a narcissistic parenting technique.

If your child expresses himself and contradicts you, the gloves come off! No child should ever criticize a parent, especially you, and you will not allow such sacrilege. Overall, your child must understand that he is not to have his own feelings—yours are the only ones that matter.

To punish any form of boat rocking, you have numerous tools at your disposal. You can show them how much they've hurt you and play the guilt card, you can throw a tantrum and intimidate them, or you can employ the silent treatment and withhold your love and affection. Finally, you can threaten to abandon your child, a remarkably effective tactic.

Stages of Narcissistic Parenting

1. **In utero:** Having a baby is all about the shower, the gifts, the cute little shoes, and choosing an appropriately weird (extra points for creative spellings!) name. Or, you may want to name your child after yourself.

2. **Infant:** People will continue to give you lots of attention for having a newborn.

Dysfunctional Dictionary

birth art: Art that depicts or celebrates a woman's individual pregnancy or childbirth, including the **belly cast**, a plaster cast of a pregnant woman's stomach that is often used to make a highly adorned ceramic sculpture for display in the home.

brag book: Small, portable photo album to show strangers, especially on airplanes and at book clubs.

gallery wall: Mass display of family photographs, often professionally taken, that remind parents of the beautiful family they've created.

holiday newsletter: Annual letter that boasts about the achievements of one's offspring, generally highly exaggerated so as to reflect well on the parents and make recipients feel inferior.

When you send out baby announcements, make sure that you pat yourself on the back for managing to procreate.

3. **Baby:** When your baby cries or expresses needs, just walk away. How annoying!

4. **Toddler:** Dress your child exactly like you, then yell if she spills on her outfit. Lock your bedroom door so your child can't disturb you if she has a nightmare.

5. **Child:** Finally—your child can get you beer from the fridge and actually pitch in around the house.

6. **Adolescent:** Apparently, your child has been put on this earth to torment you. Punish only those behaviors that irritate you, paying no attention to those that are actually bad for her.

7. **Teen:** Remove her bedroom door from its hinges—privacy is for you and you alone!

8. **Young adult:** Leave repeated phone messages calling her ungrateful and mean. Cry. When something happens in her world, make sure she knows it's worse for you.

9. **Adult:** Leave repeated phone messages calling her ungrateful and mean. Cry. When something happens in her world, make sure she knows it's worse for you.

Results for the Narcissistically Parented Child

If you work hard to make sure your children know it's all about you, there's so much to look forward to in their adulthood. Your ungrateful offspring will be characterized by the following useful traits:

- Submissive, even when someone else is abusing them.

- Seek acceptance from others, at their own expense.

- Will often enter into relationships with narcissists.

- May become narcissists themselves.

- Under- or overdeveloped boundaries.

- Strong tendencies toward codependence.

- "Mama's boys" and "Daddy's girls."

- Unsure of their own feelings and emotions; often unable to identify or modulate them.

- Dampened sense of self.

- Feelings of powerlessness or impotence.

- Drug and alcohol addiction.

- Avoid you in adulthood, possibly changing their phone numbers and moving far away.

Your Child, Your Mirror

Thank goodness you had children—they are your legacy, your genetically superior yes-men, your support system not only for your old age, but for your whole age! Yes, they're bound to let you down, but with a few strokes of manipulation, you'll have them right back where you want them—until they leave for good. For narcissists, because it's hard to maintain successful relationships, it's necessary to birth them.

Next we'll explore a parenting type that seems very different, but in fact it has much in common with the narcissist because it's all about buying or bribing your child's love. Read on as we explore the indulger!

CHAPTER 6

WHATEVER THEY WANT: INDULGENCE BEGETS ENTITLEMENT

YOU DIDN'T HAVE A CHILD TO DENY her or set limits. After all, she'll only be with you for 18 years—though it's bound to be at least 10 more, given how much she enjoys being indulged—so why spend it saying no? Enforcing boundaries is exhausting. Discipline will wear both of you down, with endless battles about doing homework, talking back, hitting, and manners. Why not just avoid the whole thing? Your child will *want* to behave because you're going to give her everything you didn't have. No pair of jeans is too expensive, even if she's still growing. Though she doesn't do her chores, you're going to dole out a hefty allowance—hey, it's the only way to stop her tantrums. If she gets into trouble in the outside world, you're going to do your best to get her out of it without accountability or apology. She's your little angel—how dare they say otherwise?

Once you commit to raising a little prince or princess who will grow up to be an entitled, boredom-stricken, unresourceful brat, you've got a failsafe parenting path for every child-hood phase. While this approach can be more expensive than others and often entails your sharing your bed with your children, there are so many rewards. We'll show you:

- Why your materialism and commitment to everything gourmet might just make this the right approach for you.

- How undeserved and constant praise will ruin your child for gainful employment.

- Why your child should never experience normal life challenges and learning experiences.

- How to get through the challenging teen years by buying your child's love.

Should You Be an Indulger?

Indulgent parents are a special breed. While they tend toward the wealthier end of the spectrum, with today's consumer credit boom, even less affluent parents can afford to buy their children whatever they want. Of course indulgence is not limited to material possessions and can be executed successfully when exclusively applied to the behavioral arena.

Many indulgent parents have waited until they were older and better established in their own lives to start their families. With their higher income bracket, work challenges, and a belief that they can execute perfect child rearing merely by reading books and paying for private schools, indulgence comes naturally to these parents. Indeed, the indulger type frequently overlaps with the neglector, since a dominant indulger subspecies is the parent who uses indulgence to compensate for spending so much time away from their children. Some indulgent parents experienced poverty in their youth, so they're proud to be able to give to their children, while others attempt to counter their strict upbringings with an atmosphere of permissiveness.

While parenting approaches like control and pushing take conscious work, indulgence is just the opposite—it's easy! You don't have to teach your children manners, morals, or a work ethic, and you avoid the unpleasantness that comes with saying no. Finally, you make it more likely that your child will like you all the time, and what could be better than that?

You will naturally gravitate toward indulgence if you exhibit any of the following characteristics, behaviors, or beliefs, whether in parenting or in other aspects of your life, such as work or marriage:

- You're lazy.

- You believe that whatever will be will be, and your job is only to watch fate unfold.

- You had kids because you came up with some great ideas for decorating the nursery.

- Only other people's children behave poorly (which, of course, is attributable to poor parenting).

Your Child Is the Center of the World

Your child's birth was the second coming, and everything stopped so you could create the perfect world for him. Every peep and every poop was sacred. When it came time to feedings and sleeping, you let him set the schedule—after all, who better knows what he needs than the infant himself?

Your job as a parent is to teach your child that the world revolves around him. To do this, always make your child's wishes the top priority. There's no such thing as give and take—for your child, there is only take, whenever he wants. If you have friends over for dinner, for example, and your child interrupts an interesting discussion, don't tell him to wait because someone else is speaking. Instead, stop everything and pay attention to your child. It's okay to make your friends feel like interlopers.

Sacrifice your marriage to your child if necessary. If your child prefers that you stay home and throws a tantrum when you plan a date night, cancel your dinner reservations and stay home. Your child should not comprehend that sometimes it's necessary to wait or that other people have pesky needs and desires—if he does, you're not doing your job.

No Limits, No Boundaries

Discipline is for mean, evil parents—not to mention that discipline is the least fun part of the parent's job! Your child will tell you when she wants to go to bed, when she wants to eat broccoli, when she wants to do schoolwork. If you're the kind of person who buys organic fruit and uses canvas grocery bags, you can justify your parenting approach as "natural."

The indulgent parent lets the child be in charge. Always give in to your child's tantrums. If her lower lip so much as quivers,

---

Dysfunctional Dictionary

kidfluence: Impact children have on their parents' purchasing decisions.

nag factor: Degree to which parents' purchasing decisions are based their children's repetitive demands.

pester power: Children's ability to persuade parents to purchase items they would not otherwise buy or perform actions they would not otherwise do.

give her what she wants. Your child should never suffer through a crying spell that lasts longer than a few seconds. On the rare occasion that you do create a rule, always be prepared to negotiate it, especially with young children, and ultimately give in. Your children will test you constantly, and you want to show them that it works.

There should be no boundaries between children and adults, neither in power and authority nor in privileges and possessions. If your child wants to sleep with you every night, scoot over and make room in between yourself and your spouse. By the time your child is an adolescent, don't subject yourself or her to the unnecessary pain of curfews and ill-informed prejudices against sex, drugs, and rock and roll.

Never Hold Your Child Accountable

It is *never* your child's fault. When your child attempts to blame someone else for a problem, encourage this resourceful response. If your child gets into trouble, whether in school, with friends, or with the law, always do whatever you can to bail him out. Nobody but you is allowed to discipline your child, and even you don't do it! You must protect your child from this type of persecution. How dare they?

Inconsistent rule enforcement is an excellent tool for the indulgent parent because it teaches children that rules aren't important as well as develops critical manipulation skills. You may find yourself mistakenly issuing punishments from time to time, but you can remedy the situation by not allowing them to stick. For example, you might threaten to take away allowance then give in when the weekend comes.

While many parents believe in assigning chores so children will learn to work hard and contribute to the family, the indulger knows that this battle isn't worth fighting, not to mention that many indulgers have housekeepers. Since your child will probably grow up to be a model, actor, professional athlete, or personal celebrity assistant, what does he need a work ethic for?

Overpraise Your Child

Your child is a beautiful, handsome, charming genius, and your job is to boost her self-esteem sky-high. Never withhold praise from your child, even if she's doing something you'd prefer that she not do. For example, if she's running all over the house like a dervish, breaking lamps and scuffing floors, praise her lightning-quick speed!

If your child is involved in an activity that requires multiple steps, praise every step of the performance rather than solely applauding the final result. This way your child will come to expect credit for even the most minor of accomplishments. Praise should be the carrot that motivates your child, not the intrinsic reward of a job well done. When your child is doing normal things that she is expected to do, praise and thank her anyway.

Undeserved, unlimited praise is one of the best ways for a parent to instill a deep sense of entitlement. When your child grows up and goes out into the world, you'll know you've done your job when she can't understand why nobody else likes her.

Start 'Em Young

Doesn't your child deserve luxury goods? Fortunately, recent years have seen a rise in items that aren't just good enough for your offspring—they're good enough for *you*!

- **Itsmybinky.com's diamond-studded pacifier:** $17,000. Because binkies never get lost.

- **Goyard diaper bag:** $3,000. Matches adult luggage set.

- **Maclaren GB Type-Au stroller:** $4,000. Black leather upholstery. Comes with 9-karat gold brooch. Motto: "What a mother wants, what a baby needs."

- **Lego life-sized Batman:** $27,000. Comes partially assembled.

- **Junior Off-Roader:** $40,000. Car for kids that includes sound system and leather seats.

- **Fantasy Coach bed:** $47,000. Just like the pre-pumpkin Cinderella model.

- **Tumble Outpost:** $97,510. Play structure for the backyard; slide included for free.

- **Custom Couture Fashion Design Kit:** $800. Kit provides materials (swatches, sketchbook) for a child to design a garment, which is then created as a one-of-a-kind outfit. Also comes in purse version.

Buy Your Child's Love

Children are becoming consumers at younger and younger ages, thanks to clever advertising campaigns that are targeted directly at your offspring. No longer is it the parents' job to introduce kids to products and materialism—if you let your child sit in front of the television for a few hours a day, he'll know what he wants soon enough. He will make his taste clear when you go to the grocery store, toy store, and mall by begging you to finance the objects of his desire.

Some parents force their children to work for their money, saving up to buy their desired nonessentials. To the indulger, this is just plain crass. Putting your child to work, as if he were household staff? The "meaning of money," which such slave driver parents quote as a lesson for their children, is that it grows on plastic trees. Your child will always be able to get money from you, well into his thirties, or from consumer credit. Why set him up with false practices that stand on outmoded principles?

Instead, you want to buy your child whatever he wants, charging it if you must. Pay no attention to whether your child craves toys that he will quickly tire of, or whether the clothing he wants is age-inappropriate. If he wants it, get it! Your job is to make sure he is never bored or insecure in comparison with his friends. Remember how important designer jeans were in your youth? *Never* allow your child to suffer the anguish of going without.

By buying your child whatever he wants, he will love you more. You will be able to direct his behavior with bribes, and he will learn that he must behave to receive presents. Save up a list of things you know he wants so that when you need him to do something he doesn't feel like doing, you can dangle one of them as incentive. Because your child has the best toys, clothes, and food, other children will want to play at your house. Kids like stuff, and they like doing what they want to do. As an indulger parent, your kids will like you all the time!

Stages of Indulgence

1. **In utero:** Decorate the nursery with stuffed animals and toys your child will

---

Tidings of Trauma

"All I've *got* at home is two dogs and four cats and six bunny rabbits and two parakeets and three canaries and a green parrot and a turtle and a bowl of goldfish and a cage of white mice and a silly old hamster! I want a *squirrel!*"

—Veruca Salt, in Roald Dahl's *Charlie and the Chocolate Factory*

---

not need for years. Buy multiple cute outfits for your child to grow into.

2. **Infant:** Don't put your child on any kind of sleep or eating schedule.

3. **Baby:** Whenever your child cries, pick her up.

4. **Toddler:** If your toddler has a tantrum, give her whatever she wants. Rather than asking her to help you pick up her toys, clean up after her. No bedtime.

5. **Child:** Take your child to malls and toy stores and let her have whatever she wants. If she wants you to stay home with her when you have plans, cancel your plans. No bedtime.

6. **Adolescent:** Allow your child to attend concerts and stay out late. Don't put any limits on her television watching. If her

grades suffer, bribe her with clothing or electronics, or just let the grades slip.

7. **Teen:** Your child will probably not want to participate in any family activities, such as dinner or gatherings. Let her do whatever she wants, and don't enforce any kind of curfew.

8. **Young adult:** Whenever your child gets into trouble, bail her out. Send her money whenever she requests it.

9. **Adult:** Don't ask your child to move out at any age. Give her money whenever she requests it.

Results for the Indulged Child

If you put effort toward indulging your child's every whim, there's so much to look forward to in their adulthood. Your gourmet offspring will be characterized by the following entitled traits:

- Chronic boredom thanks to never having learned to entertain themselves.

- Low tolerance for frustration.

- Demanding and self-centered.

- Face a harsh reality when they get into outside world without parents to pave the way.

- Bosses will hate them because they think they're special without having to work for anything.

- Believe rules don't apply to them.

- Don't respect other people's rights.

- Try to control people; manipulative.

- Don't know the difference between needs and wants.

- Insist on having their own way.

- Poor money-management skills.

- Whiners.

- Dependent on parents into adulthood.

The Happily Spoiled Child

Your child never wants to hear you say no, and you really don't want to say it. Make both of you happy by pulling it from your vocabulary! You and your child are only on this earth for a short time, and you can't take it with you. Don't both of you deserve the best and the easiest?

Next we're going to have a look at a parenting type that dovetails nicely with the indulger—in fact, if you were to cross narcissism with indulgence, you just might get the best friend!

CHAPTER 7

WE SHARE EVERYTHING: PARENT AS BEST FRIEND

AH, THE BEST-FRIEND PARENT.
Closely aligned with the narcissist and the
indulger, the best-friend parent is fortunate
to have all her needs met by her child. All
social woes pre-childbirth—lack of popular-
ity, difficulty forging close adult relationships, problematic marriages—are solved
for the best-friend parent after the children
come along. "Mini-me" is too flat a phrase to
describe these junior companions—they are
confidantes and shoulders to lean on, com-
patriots in fun and partners in crime. There
are no boundaries between the best-friend
parent and her child, who go everywhere
together and share everything. Whether it's

dancing to the same music or smoking from the same joint, the best-friend parent and her precocious offspring exemplify togetherness. If you're interested in having a best friend for life, in this chapter we'll show you:

- How your child can be an excellent sounding board for marital problems or sexual dilemmas.

- Why you don't need to pursue any other relationships after you have kids.

- How to stay hip and fun so your kids will like you.

- Why you should withhold affection if your child threatens you with independence.

Should You Be a Best Friend?

Does much of your identity derive from perceiving yourself as fun, hip, and young at heart? Do you love the idea of having a constant companion who's dependent on you for affection and support? If so, you may be an ideal candidate for the best-friend parent.

Best-friend parents tend to cluster in a few categories. Some didn't enjoy their own social lives as children and teens, and revel in the opportunity to reinvent themselves through their own children, while others look upon their own youths as glory days and try to stay in that headspace for as long as possible. Some think of themselves as hip despite their advanced years and feel they can stay that way by relating to their kids, thus reversing their own experience of fuddy-duddy parents. Many didn't enjoy their distanced relationships with their parents and vow not to repeat that mistake.

Best-friend parents value honesty above all else. No information should be filtered just because a child is, well, a child—instead, they're pre-adults who are going to discover the harsh truth anyway, so why not hear it from their parents? Those suited to the best-friend role think very highly of their own children and assess them as peers, professing pride in their kids' being "mature for their age"—after all, they made them that way!

You will naturally gravitate toward best-friend parenting if you exhibit any of the following characteristics, behaviors, or beliefs, whether in parenting or in other aspects of your life, such as work or marriage:

- In other relationships, you've been accused of being clingy or needy, with your identity becoming submerged.

- When you're walking around downtown or at the mall, you more frequently

admire what the kids are wearing than
the outfits sported by people your age.

- You are relieved at the prospect of no
  longer having to manage your own
  social life.

- You really, really, really want your kids
  to like you.

Share Everything with Your Child

The mantra of the best-friend parent is "no
boundaries." When you have a child, you've
bred a confidante. It's so important that you
be able to share everything with your best
friend, a relationship that could suffer were

you to keep any secrets. Whether the topic is finances or sex, be as explicit as possible with your child—preferably while sharing a glass of Chardonnay.

The more you discuss adult issues with your child, the more he will become adept at navigating them with you. Soon enough he'll be giving you marital advice, if you're married, or commiserating with you over the problems of your ex, if you're no longer together. Just as you would discuss acquaintances in common with a regular friend, so can you parse the vagaries of marriage and divorce with your child.

Take your child everywhere with you. Even if wedding invitations state "No Children," assume they were referring to all the *other* children, not your little precious. If you've got poker night, bring the kid. If you're off to the nail salon, make sure she gets her fingers and toes painted to. Even strip clubs are more fun when the kids come along.

Given that you like to stay out late, your child won't need a bedtime. Not only will you save money on babysitters, everybody at the bar will comment on how cute your child is—just like a little grown-up!

Allow Your Other Relationships to Suffer

When you entered your marriage (if indeed you started your family that way), you probably had the romantic notion that wedded bliss would meet all your needs—until you had your first child. No relationship you'd experienced until then could match this new bond, and suddenly your spouse seemed so inadequate. This is a great start to a best-friend bond with your kids. Don't fall prey to such divisive elements as "date night" with your spouse, or marital counseling. Let the chips fall where they may, and hopefully at some point the spouse will be out of the picture so that you and the kids can discuss what a problem he or she was. Obviously, whether or not you stay married, your child will always take your side.

Dysfunctional Dictionary

askable parent: Parent who encourages and is willing to answer questions about sex and other adult topics.

MILF: From "*m*other *I'*d *l*ike to *f*uck," a term characterizing sexually appealing mothers (especially those who can attract much younger men or their children's friends), particularly those who put youthful effort into their appearance: going to the gym, maintaining a tan, seeking plastic surgery, and dressing in the latest fashions. Also **yummy mummy** and **Stacy's Mom**.

rejuvenile: Adult who enjoys activities normally associated with children.

While you may have had a thriving social life before your children were born, after their arrival, don't put any effort into keeping up with your friends. This will probably happen naturally if you insist on bringing your children with you wherever you go. When your kids are older, you'll be hanging out with their friends, anyway.

Let Your Children Know You're Dependent on Them

Now that there's no competition for your affection, you will be entirely dependent on your children for social sustenance. Make sure they know this. When you relate to your child as a surrogate spouse, using her to fill in the emptiness you feel, make sure she knows she's deserting you if she wants to do something without you. Ask if you can join, and if not, break down into tears and

say, "But you're the only one who loves me!"
Let them know that someday they will have
to support you, and mention how happy you
will be when they give you grandchildren
you can be friends with someday.

Join Your Child's Trends

Your child will keep you young! As a
parent, you're fortunate that you've got
a living, breathing trend-spotter coming
home to you every day. All you have to do
is observe and plan lots of shopping trips
together. If your child wears her thong way
above the waistband of her jeans, so should
you! If your child wants a tattoo, get ones
that match! Share music with your child so
you can rock out together. When your child
shares the latest slang with you, remember
to incorporate it into your speech. Nothing's
better than a 50-year-old who says "Dude."

Overall, your goal is to become such a buddy that you lose your parental authority, which functions as a final frontier separating you from your best-friend child. One thing that is sure to help obliterate this dysfunctional barrier is partying with your child. Not only is it safer for your child to experiment with alcohol and drugs with you rather than out on the streets, it's more fun for you! Between the two of you, your kid probably has better access to dealers than you do, and you've got that over-21 driver's license—what a team!

Punish Your Child Only for Being a Bad Friend

Many parents ruin their friendships with their children by forcing them to do things they don't want to do, like homework. As a parent, you've got to pick and choose your battles, and the ones to avoid are those that may compromise the possibility of your children liking you. Just as you wouldn't boss around a peer, best-friend parents don't give rules or tell their children what to do.

The exception to this hands-off approach to parenting, however, is when your child behaves like a bad friend—not inviting you to join a party, leaving you in the lurch on a

---

I've Got Your Back

Baseball games are celebrated as occasions for male bonding, a place where the parental relationship can be infused with friendship. Chicago Cubs fan William Ligue Jr., for example, took offense at the Kansas City Royals first-base coach, so he and his 15-year-old son (both shirtless) jumped down from the stands to attack him. Following this special father-son moment, Ligue stated: "I just want to thank God for giving me the courage to do this with my son tonight. Thanks, Lord, I owe you one."

Friday or Saturday night, neglecting to tell you an important secret, failing to wash your jeans after he's borrowed them. In these instances, crack down hard with the silent treatment, and sooner or later he'll realize what it takes to be a good friend.

Stages of Best-Friend Parenting

1. **In utero:** Start buying paraphernalia for all the things you'd like to do with your child, like a baseball mitt.

2. **Infant:** Call your child "little buddy." Start talking to your child about your feelings, even though she can't understand what you're saying.

3. **Baby:** Make sure your child still sleeps in your bed, at least through toddlerhood. Whenever your child cries, run to her, saying "I'll never leave you!"

4. **Toddler:** Buy identical outfits for yourself and your child to wear. Decline to enroll your child in preschool—that would be too much time away from you!

5. **Child:** Now that your child is ambulatory and verbal, you truly can do everything together. Take your child out of school some days just so the two of you can do fun stuff!

6. **Adolescent:** Start getting to know your child's friends. When she has sleepovers, stay up late with the gang and get them to confide in you about things they'd never tell their own parents. Do whatever it takes to be identified as the "fun one."

7. **Teen:** Introduce your child to drinking and drugs, if that's what you enjoy doing, or at the very least, condone it because it's cool!

8. **Young adult:** Resent the fact that your child may be striking out on her own, and stage mini-breakdowns to bring her back to your side.

9. **Adult:** Do whatever you can to make your child move back in with you and tell her that neither of you needs anybody else.

Results for the Child of the Best Friend

If you manage to forge a best-friendship with your children, there's so much to look forward to in their adulthood. Created in your image, your best friends will be characterized by the following appealing traits:

- Either utterly without emotional boundaries, or with thick walls up to protect themselves from parental intrusions.

Parents Make the Party!

When you buy alcohol for your kids, not only do you make sure they're getting it from a safe source, you get to join in on the fun! According to a 2005 American Medical Association study, almost 25 percent of teens have been supplied alcohol by their own parents and 40 percent by a friend's parent. Among the adults, 25 percent of the parents feel that teens should be able to drink at home with their parents present.

- Terrified at having too much control over their parents.

- Resentful that they had to grow up too quickly.

- Sexually promiscuous.

- Doubtful about the viability of marriage and close romantic relationships.

- Impaired work ethic, lack of discipline.

- Addicted to alcohol or drugs.

BFF!

"Best friends forever!" What could be better? Not only is this child flesh of your flesh, you'll never have to worry about social awkwardness again. The best-friend parenting type is one of the easiest to make up as you go along—just treat your child as you would an actual friend!

Next we turn to something completely different. In fact, you could even characterize it as "parent as enemy": the self-esteem killer. For those who have chosen the best-friend type, read on so you'll know what *not* to do. For others, however, this type will mesh perfectly with their unique parenting instincts!

CHAPTER 8
VALIDATION IS FOR PARKING: KILLING SELF-ESTEEM

LIFE IS TOUGH, AND THE SOONER your child figures out he's nothing special, the better. There's no free lunch, and you're not doing him any favors by falsely building up his touchy-feely self-esteem just so he can get it crushed in the real world. After all, you didn't get a leg up, so why should he? Some children think the universe revolves around them, but what about the rude awakening when they get a job and their boss tells them the truth—that they're worthless? Better that he be prepared by having his family inform him he's worthless throughout his childhood, so by the time it comes from a stranger, he'll have a thick skin. Once you commit to parenting via self-esteem homicide, you'll not only bestow a great gift on your offspring, you'll have a punching bag for the inevitable stresses of your own life. In this chapter, we'll show you:

- Why you should ridicule your child's flaws and fears.

- How to set up expectations your child could never possibly fulfill, so that failure is inevitable.

- Why imagination is for sissies.

- Why your children will never amount to anything.

Should You Be a Self-Esteem Killer?

As a self-esteem killer, you will have a special kinship with your children because you yourself have low self-esteem. Whether or not you're entirely aware of it, you loathe yourself deeply, a gift you plan to share with your child. Life has been a huge disappointment for you, and your child is no exception. Fortunately, she's young and can't defend herself, so she makes a perfect target for your pent-up feelings of failure. For most of her childhood, she won't strike back at you, and indeed will confirm your superficial delusions of grandeur by returning put-downs with love. Unlike most of the people in your life, your child will believe you when you tell her how inadequate she is.

In general, parents' and children's self-esteem parallel one another, so the self-esteem killer is an ideal parenting choice for someone whose own parents killed their self-esteem. Self-esteem homicide tends to carry forward as a family legacy, so your own parents should be proud to see you carry on the family tradition!

Because the brief feelings of power that come with putting your children down don't last, this parenting type develops its own momentum. As with any deliberate parenting type, killing self-esteem takes work, but with the minimum of effort you'll find that it's easier and easier to spontaneously make your child feel terrible about herself.

Self-esteem homicide cross-pollinates beautifully with the controller, the pusher, the narcissist, and the neglector, so be sure to examine those sections for ways to deepen your ability to crush your child's spirit. You will naturally gravitate toward self-esteem killing if you exhibit any of the following characteristics, behaviors, or beliefs, whether in parenting or in other aspects of your life, such as work or marriage:

- You have horrible luck. Others do nothing and get everything, while you have an inferior life that you didn't even choose.

Promoting Sibling Rivalry

While parents play the key role in killing their children's self-esteem, siblings can also be enlisted in the effort. Here are some helpful guidelines for pitting siblings against one another:

1. Compare them to one another, especially unfavorably (e.g., "Why aren't you as smart as your brother?").

2. Pigeonhole them. One child could be "the pretty one," for example, while another is "the funny one."

3. Don't treat them as individuals; instead, push all of them to excel at the same activities (then compare them, as suggested in tip 1).

4. Pick favorites. Every parent has one, so it's simply a matter of enacting the favoritism.

5. Avoid alone time with individual children, except when reinforcing favoritism.

6. Don't interfere in sibling fights, even if the older, larger sibling is physically attacking the younger, smaller sibling.

- Everybody is out to get you.

- If only people acted right, you'd be able to relax.

- Your own parents didn't coddle you, that's for sure.

Constantly Criticize, Never Praise

To toughen your child's skin and induce him to shape up, it's important to direct him with criticism. By all appearances, you've been cursed with a bumbling, stupid, ugly child. How dare he subject you to such inadequacy? The only way to get him back on track is to criticize him frequently and withhold praise. Criticism is best delivered in front of others, whether family, friends, or in public places, because humiliation will help your child learn.

Compare your child unfavorably to others, including siblings, friends, and people on television. Helpful words include "worthless," "good for nothing," and "idiot," especially when presented in a mocking tone. Let your child know that he can't do anything right so there are now cracks in the negativity of his self-image. Never allow him to live down his mistakes, reminding him of them long after they've occurred. When in groups, regale others with stories of your child's idiocy; include a few such tales in your holiday family newsletter.

It practically goes without saying that praise is anathema to this parenting type. While it will require some self-control for you to refrain from making any positive pronouncements, remember that you're doing it all for your child; soon there will be no risk of accidentally saying anything nice.

Don't Cut Your Child Any Slack

Just because your child is young doesn't
mean she shouldn't be accountable for her
ideas and actions. By knocking her down
from the start, she will learn to question
her own thoughts and understand that
her opinions don't matter. If your child has
an idea that's derivative or overly obvious, don't excuse it by saying it's smart
"for a child." If it's dumb, it's dumb! When
your child spills her orange juice, instead
of chalking up her clumsiness to a lack of
knowledge about gravity combined with
undeveloped motor-muscle control, go ballistic and call her a clumsy oaf. If you begin

making excuses for your child today, when will it stop? When she's a convicted felon?

Imagination Is an Unaffordable Luxury

When you're on the job, bringing home the bacon, do you have time or energy to exercise your imagination? Probably not. Life is hard and it demands pragmatic, realistic thinking, not tangerine trees and marmalade skies. You don't do your child any favors by encouraging sissy thinking. Besides, it's not like you can tell that drawing is of a horse, anyway.

Children have ridiculous senses of humor. They like knock-knock jokes and armpit-hand farting, and they can giggle about nothing for hours on end. Nip this in the bud by rolling your eyes or you'll find yourself with a kid who thinks he's better than everybody else. When your child comes to you requesting music or dance lessons, remind him that he can't carry a tune and there's no money for such frippery. Children are always developing interests that fade quickly, or worse, last a lifetime. Don't encourage him.

Curiously, the lower your child's self-esteem, the more likely it is he will become a writer.

You're Fat, You're Ugly

While physical attributes may not be the most important thing in the universe, we live in a looks-oriented world, and you never get a second chance to make a first impression. How badly it reflects on you to have a child who's less than perfect!

In order to encourage her to keep up her looks, let her know what a disappointment she is to you. Whether it's acne, weight, bad hair, poor taste, facial features, or the ravages of puberty, impress upon your child how she fails to measure up in the looks department.

In this day and age, weight is the most important personal characteristic, more significant than character, morals, virtue, or intelligence. At the same time, child-hood obesity is epidemic. Make sure your child knows that it is her number-one job to stay thin (whether or not you're able to accomplish this). You'd rather her grades suffer than her weight increase. Put her on a diet, restrict her favorite foods, and never pass up the opportunity to tell her she's a fat, unlovable slob.

Predict a Terrible Future

Happiness has been defined as the gap between expectation and reality. Your child will never amount to anything, so why set him up for disappointment? Whenever possible, remind your child that he has nothing to look forward to. Useful phrases include "You're worthless," "You'll never amount to anything," and "You're a complete disappointment to me." Someday your child will turn to you and say, "You were right all along." What a proud moment!

Stages of Self-Esteem Murder

1. **In utero:** Allow yourself to feel irritated at the inconveniences of pregnancy, reminding yourself that the baby is willfully causing indigestion, nausea, and sleeplessness (for mothers), not to

Don't Raise a Fatty

Who wants an overweight child? Fortunately, parents have a real head start in promoting the cult of thin—kids themselves. Almost half of girls in the first through third grades report wanting to be thinner. By their teens, half of girls and a quarter of boys have tried dieting. Of the girls, one in three don't even need to lose weight! Best of all, teens with low self-esteem are more likely to diet, so any preexisting self-esteem-killing parenting will only help further the cause. While children and teens who diet are far more likely to be overweight within five years as well as have disordered eating habits, at least by then they'll be out of the house and on their own.

mention inflicting a fat, whiny wife (for fathers). Wonder why the ultrasound depicts such an ugly fetus.

2. **Infant:** Tell your child to stop being such a crybaby and wrinkle your nose in disgust when you must finally change a rancid diaper.

3. **Baby:** When your child spits up, yell at him for making a mess.

4. **Toddler:** With their clumsiness and tantrums, it's not hard to find plenty of opportunities to tell toddlers they're idiots.

5. **Child:** Once your child is in school, you can begin comparing him to others and gathering tangible proof of his stupidity.

6. **Adolescent:** Puberty brings physical changes that make any person look ugly—make sure these do not pass uncommented.

7. **Teen:** In the teen years, referring to your child's bleak, useless future is especially effective.

8. **Young adult:** While watching your child flounder in the early stages of adulthood, say "I told you so" whenever possible.

9. **Adult:** Now that he's fully grown, let your child know there's no longer any doubt that he's a huge disappointment.

Results for the Child with No Self-Esteem

If you work hard to instill poor self-esteem in your children, there's so much to look forward to in their adulthood. Your self-hating offspring will be characterized by the following useful traits:

- Depressed, withdrawn, pessimistic.

- Fear of trying new things due to possible failure.

- Easily frustrated.

- Unable to find solutions for problems.

- Blame others for their problems.

- Exhibit "learned helplessness," passivity that results from repeated exposure to negative feedback and lack of belief in the possibility of making anything better.

- Quitters.

- Susceptible to peer pressure.

- Can become bullies in order to vent their negative feelings.

- Suicidal.

- Addicted to drugs and alcohol.

Self-Fulfilling Prophesies

The beauty of the self-esteem-killing approach is that it begets itself. While in your child's early years you will find yourself doing much of the work, but soon enough she'll believe exactly what you tell her, and the burden of repeatedly telling her that she's worthless will dissipate.

In the next chapter, we will explore the seventh and final traumatic parenting type, the neglector. While the self-esteem killer actively instills negativity children, the neglector can achieve similar results, as the effect of parental absence on children makes them feel unlovable.

CHAPTER 9
DON'T QUIT YOUR DAY JOB:
THE CONVENIENCE OF NEGLECT

LIFE IS A COMPLICATED BUSINESS. So many parents are busy working, socializing, or languishing under the bedcovers. Since it's likely that they themselves were neglected, these parents know that childhood neglect is no big deal. Even for those who weren't neglected, however, it's possible to learn and embrace these handy techniques, especially for fathers. When you neglect your children, you show them that they're not worthy of time or affection. In this vein, the results of neglect mimic low self-esteem. Neglected children will learn to fend for themselves, sometimes reversing roles with their parents. For example, if you're a drinker, it's likely you can get your child to take care of *you*! There's no denying that neglect is the easiest parenting type there is, characterized not by the presence of behaviors you'll have to learn but instead by absence both physical and emotional. In this chapter, we'll show you all the tools for this prevalent approach, including:

- Why kissing and hugging should be avoided.

- How to keep your children from knowing the real you.

- Why it's so important to choose work over school plays and sporting events.

- How to hire others to handle parenting duties for you.

Should You Be a Neglector?

So many individuals are well suited to be neglectful parents. Some neglectors choose addiction over their children. Others are depressed and emotionally unable to cope with the pressures of parenting. And many are so caught up in the rat race of career and social climbing that they don't feel they can take time to perform parenting functions themselves, deciding instead to outsource the work.

As with all the types, if you yourself were raised in the way you would like to parent (i.e., if you were neglected), you're going to have an easier time adopting the type's techniques. Neglectors tend to have difficulty with intimacy, uncomfortable with revealing themselves to or becoming dependent upon others. They can feel overwhelmed with the challenges of everyday life, feeling that the pressures of parenting bring yet another set of undesirable responsibilities. Sometimes they are enthusiasts who believe that every activity should be characterized by quality over quantity; after spreading themselves too thin, they convince themselves that parenting can take place in small, concentrated spurts. Overall, neglector parents tend to be self-absorbed and lack emotional maturity.

You will naturally gravitate toward neglect if you exhibit any of the following characteristics, behaviors, or beliefs, whether in parenting or in other aspects of your life, such as work or marriage:

Tidings of Trauma

"The place of the father in the modern suburban family is a very small one, particularly if he plays golf."
—Bertrand Russell

- It always seems like people want more from you than you're willing to give.

- You continually pledge to make significant changes after the next hurdle but never do so.

- You're already neglecting your spouse.

- You don't believe that children should affect your lifestyle.

Building Invisible Walls

Children are naturally affectionate, so in the early stages, it's important to communicate a "hands-off" message. Soon enough they'll absorb this ethos and keeping them away from you will be effortless. Hugging and kissing should always be kept to a minimum; not only is it uncomfortable for you, it breeds sissies and may cause taboo sexual tension.

The term "crybaby," of course, comes from children's tendency to cry easily over trivial injuries both real and perceived. If you give them attention for every little scratch, they won't develop the ability to soothe themselves. When you're busy, you're busy, and it's never too early for children to learn that they need to keep their problems to themselves if you're in the middle of something.

While at times it may feel difficult to deny your children affection, remind yourself that the walls you build today will turn into tomorrow's fortress around their hearts, so impenetrable that adult intimacy will prove all but impossible.

Emotional Disengagement

In addition to withholding affection from your children, it's vital to keep them feeling that they don't know who you really are. Parents should be mysteries to their children, inscrutable and unpredictable ships passing in the night. Whenever the opportunity arises to reveal yourself to your child, squelch that urge. If your child sees you as a human being, with feelings and softness, not only will he take advantage of you at every turn, you'll never have the chance of seeming like a superhero in your child's eyes. In a tough world, empathy is for chumps, and you need to set the right hardhearted example for your offspring, giving them room to learn and grow on their own.

Someone Has to Bring Home the Bacon

Children have no concept of the realities of life. Where do they think food comes from? Who do they think pays the rent?

Dysfunctional Dictionary

cot potato: Baby or toddler who logs many hours in front of the television.

manny: Male nanny.

nanny envy: Parental jealousy over the amount of time the nanny gets to spend with the children.

screenager: Child who has grown up with screens, especially televisions and computers.

virtual visit: Child-parent interaction via webcams.

While they're whining about their needs, do they ever acknowledge all your efforts? Reconcile yourself to the fact that your children will never appreciate all that you do. When you stay late at work or your frequent business travel causes you to miss yet another school event, assuage your guilt by congratulating yourself for being a good provider. It's not like you left them with nothing to do: they've got the television, video games, and computers to keep them occupied. If they complain, tell them they're ungrateful brats.

Everybody Needs "Me" Time

Because your life is stressful, you must put your needs first. Whether it's frequent vacations, a frenetic social life, time spent cultivating high-level hygiene, or merely the servicing of an addiction, you need frequent breaks from your children to stay sane. Someday, when they're parents themselves, they'll understand what it's like. In the meantime, don't reject any opportunities or change your lifestyle in order to be a parent. Because children lack perspective, they will never understand your needs, so it's up to you to honor them.

Outsourced Parenting

Fortunately for the neglector, there are many resources to make sure that children don't harm themselves in your absence. With a wide range of options as well as costs, you're certain to find the solution that's right for you.

For the affluent, nannies and boarding school are excellent options. Live-in nannies provide far more childcare for the investment and save you from having to schedule different babysitters for evening outings. In many cases, children end up preferring their nannies, which takes pressure off parents. While in the United States boarding school is less common than in England, there are still plenty of possibilities for all kinds of children, whether you need disciplinary action or just more time off.

Those who can't afford full-time help or boarding schools often use daycare. Most preschools and childcare facilities offer extra services to extend your child's stay, so you can cobble together as many as twelve daily hours to have the kids off your hands. You can also try leaving your children with friends, neighbors, or relatives, whether regularly or on an ad hoc basis. Even if you don't return when you say you will, these caregivers will rarely turn your child out onto the streets.

Finally, money and television make excellent providers. As outlined in the indulger parenting type, if you buy your child anything he wants, he should manage to entertain himself reasonably well. Most children have the resources to spend hours in front of the television, so if you want to go out for a while, just put the remote in their hands

Better Living Through Chemistry

Does your child run wild around the house? Do you have trouble keeping up with his antics? Is he sad, moody, or "creative"? Rather than spending unnecessary time with your child, give yourself a break and let modern medication step in.

- **Your child will fit in with his peers.** 6 to 8 million American children, or 10 to 13 percent, take daily medication for a mental health issue. Of those, 3.5 million are taking stimulants for ADHD. In 2002, doctors wrote 11 million prescriptions for antidepressants for teenagers and children, almost 8 percent of the total.

- **Your child will be patriotic.** Outside the United States, families aren't availing themselves of these resources. In the United Kingdom, for example, only 0.3 percent of children are on ADHD stimulants, while the figure is 1.4 percent in Germany and 1.2 percent in Israel.

- **They're easy to get.** Between 1994 and 2001, the number of doctor visits by adolescents that resulted in the prescription of a psychotropic medication increased 250 percent. One-third of all office visits by adolescents now leads to an ADHD diagnosis. As many as a quarter of the visits where psychotropic medications are prescribed don't even have an associated mental health diagnosis!

and show them how to help themselves to soda from the fridge.

Stages of Neglect

1. **In utero:** Don't bother changing your diet or smoking, drinking, and drug habits just because you're pregnant. For fathers, pregnancy is an ideal time to leave without a forwarding address.

2. **Infant:** Because your child can't yet get herself out of the crib, go out and run some errands when you've put her down for a nap. If you run in to a friend, find a café or bar and settle in for a long chat!

3. **Baby:** Babies can be very demanding. Use this opportunity to set your child straight by letting her know that crying will get her nowhere.

4. **Toddler:** Toddlerhood marks the beginning of a lifelong love affair with the television. Because there aren't enough hours of children's programming, get your toddler started on adult shows as early as possible.

5. **Child:** Finally—your child can feed herself and move around the neighborhood on her own two feet. Let her.

6. **Adolescent:** Only discipline your adolescent if she annoys you; otherwise, let her explore the world on her own. Chances are she'll be out of the house more often than she's at home, making adolescence a very freeing time for the parent.

7. **Teen:** For the wealthy, boarding school is now an option. Or you can try juvenile detention facilities, which are free.

8. **Young adult:** Now that your child is on her own, make some demands on her, whether for money or respect.

9. **Adult:** Watch with pride as your child neglects her own children!

Results for the Neglected Child

If you do very little to raise your children, there's so much to look forward to in their adulthood. Your laissez faire offspring will be characterized by the following inimitable traits:

- Needy and dependent, or problems with intimacy and emotional attachments.

- Grow up too fast, experiment with sex and drugs.

- Low self-esteem, feeling unworthy of love or happiness.

- Attention-seeking troublemakers.

- Seek out withholding, emotionally absent relationships.

- Anger issues, frequent fighting, aggressive.

- Depressed.

- Caretaking at the expense of self-care.

- Problems with discipline and work ethic.

- Pessimistic.

- Drug and alcohol addiction, eating disorders.

After Childbirth, Your Job Is Done!

You gave them life—what more do they want? There's work to do and life to be enjoyed. Fortunately, when you neglect

School Away from Home

For the busy parent, boarding school is an excellent way to balance lifestyle with the demands of a child. When children go away to school, they are only underfoot during holidays and occasional weekends, when it's possible to find babysitters for much of the time.

Most people think of boarding school as an alternative only for teens, but in the United States, boarding schools start at the third-grade level. This is more in keeping with the British tradition, which has always started early; nowadays, many British institutions accept seven-year-olds.

Why wait until a child is a discipline problem requiring military or wilderness school? Tuition and board may average almost $60,000 per year, but the freedom parents gain is priceless.

your children, they learn compensatory techniques for self-sufficiency, and in the meantime, you get to accomplish everything you set out to do. Restraint is the name of this game, and after some practice, you'll be withholding with the best of them.

Congratulations on taking this journey through the seven traumatic parenting types. Parenting is the toughest job you'll ever love, but now that you're equipped with the knowledge to traumatize your children deliberately, there's no end to the possibilities.

YOU THOUGHT THIS DAY WOULD never come: your children are grown and out of the house (or, in some cases, still living with you into their thirties and forties). While parenting is truly a lifelong endeavor, the critical period of responsibility is behind you. No longer do you need to focus on inflicting trauma—instead, you can sit back and watch the results unfold. Raising children is like growing a garden: you have no idea what the oak tree is going to look like when you plant the acorn in the soil. In your old age, however, you've earned the privilege of sitting in the leafy shade, and, if you've done the job correctly, you can hammer nails in the tree in order to install the treehouse of your retirement, or you can allow your children to destroy you for firewood.

Never Explain, Never Justify

All children look back on their childhood and wish their parents had done something differently. No matter the traumatizing approach you chose, your children will wish you'd gone another way, especially when they enter therapy. Don't give in to this kind of Monday-morning quarterbacking. Hindsight is 20-20, and it's all too easy to close the barn door after the horse has left the stable.

Deflect Blame

When your children complain about something you did years ago, *never* take

> ## Tidings of Trauma
>
> "Parents wonder why the streams are bitter, when they themselves have poisoned the fountain."
>
> —John Locke

responsibility for it. If you want to seem insightful, take the blame for something irrelevant that never actually affected them, but tell them you have no idea why they're whining about whatever it is that seems to matter to them. Finally, try returning the blame to them—if they hadn't been so stupid, shallow, or disobedient, you wouldn't have had to do what you did.

Remind Them of Their Responsibilities to *You*

Now that they're adults, it's time for your children to cut you some slack and start supporting you. This is cycle of life—just as you or the nanny changed their diapers, so one day will they change yours. Guilt is an excellent tool for instilling this type of responsibility—inflict it as heavily as possible, reminding them repeatedly of how much you sacrificed for them.

Don't Be Offended If They Choose a Different Approach

It's the nature of parenting that your children are likely to choose a different approach to traumatizing when they themselves have families. While at first blush it's

> ### Tidings of Trauma
>
> "Like all parents, my husband and I just do the best we can, and hold our breath, and hope we've set aside enough money to pay for our kids' therapy."
> —Michelle Pfeiffer

easy to be offended that they didn't think highly enough of your choices to repeat them, remember that once upon a time you read this book and carefully selected a traumatizing style for yourself. Rather than lambasting their unique choice, revel in parental pride for instilling in your children the traumatizing instinct. Your grandchildren will thank you one day!